Foods

from the Bible

. . . . .

by JOANNE ASALA

Contents

*The quotes in
this book are
from the King
James version
of the Bible.*

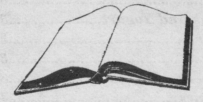

Introduction

For the Lord thy God bringeth thee into a good land, a land of brooks of water, of fountains and depths that spring out of valleys and hills; a land of wheat and barley, and vines, and fig trees, and pomegranates; a land of olive oil, and honey; a land wherein thou shalt eat bread without scarceness, thou shalt not lack anything...
– Deuteronomy 8:7-9

The land God chose for his people was a country rich in promise, where food was varied and abundant. Nearly every book in the Bible provides hints as to what these foods were and how our early ancestors grew, prepared and consumed them. Now you can recreate some of these delicious meals in your own home.

Some of these recipes have evolved over the thousands of years of Middle Eastern cuisine. Some are for meals that were enjoyed by the early inhabitants of the area – the Israelites, the Romans, the Egyptians and others. The more modern recipes have come to be recognized as regional specialties – hummus, couscous and sweetened dates to name but a few.

Yet even the more recent additions rely on the wholesome foods of the biblical era by using many of the same ingredients.

Baklava, a traditional dessert made of nuts and honey found in nearly every Middle Eastern nation, is little different from the honey cakes King David once enjoyed.

This book will show how some of our food traditions have descended from these early days of human history. I hope that by partaking of these biblical feasts, you will in some way feel closer to the people and places mentioned in the Scriptures.

Next time you eat barley bread, you may remember that Jesus fed the multitudes with five loaves of just such a bread. Or you may try Jacob's Pottage and think about how Esau once gave up his birthright for a bowl of this steaming stew.

Dietary Restrictions

Throughout the biblical era, the dietary needs of the people evolved and changed. Here is a summary of the dietary restrictions found in the Old Testament and how those restrictions were lifted through the sacrifice of Jesus.

In the Beginning, God Instituted a Vegetarian Diet

> And God said, Behold, I have given ye every herb bearing seed, which is upon the face of all the earth, and every tree, in the which is the fruit of a tree yielding seed; to ye it shall be for meat.
>
> – Genesis 1:29

At the dawn of time when man still lived in the Garden of Eden, he lived in harmony with nature and did not eat his fellow creatures. Even after Adam and Eve ate the fruit of the Tree of Knowledge and were cursed to earn their bread "by the sweat" of their brow, no mention is made of eating meat.

After the Flood, Meat Is Included

It is told that Cain was a tiller of the ground and his brother Abel a keeper of sheep. It is also mentioned how Lamech and his wife Adah had a son named Jabal who was the father of "such as have cattle." While such clues may indicate that people ate meat as soon as they left Paradise, we don't know for sure. Some scholars indicate that these animals were raised for sacrifice alone. When Noah is instructed to load up the ark,

7

he is to take only two of each animal on board so that he may "keep them alive" during the voyage. Separate instructions are given for provisions. God wants Noah to "take thou unto thee of all food that is eaten, and thou shalt gather it to thee; and it shall be for food for thee, and for them." (Genesis 6:21)

After the flood waters receded, God says to Noah:

> *And the fear of you and the dread of you shall be upon every beast of the earth, and upon every fowl of the air, upon all that moveth upon the earth, and upon all the fishes of the sea; into your hand are they delivered. Every moving thing that liveth shall be meat for you; even as the green herb have I given you all things. But flesh with the life thereof, which is the blood thereof, shall ye not eat.*
>
> – Genesis 9:2-4

God has expanded man's diet to now include "every moving thing that liveth." Whereas animals once lived in harmony with man, they were now fair game. The only prohibition at this point is that man shall not eat the blood of animals, for blood is the life force of all living creatures. Blood is only to be given up in sacrifice to God for the atonement of sins.

> *And surely your blood of your lives will I require; at the hand of every beast will I require it, and at the hand of man; at the hand of every man's brother will I require the life of man.*
>
> – Genesis 9:5

Old Testament Dietary Laws

And Moses came and told the people all the words of the Lord, and all the judgments: and all the people answered with one voice, and said, All the words which the Lord hath said will we do.

– Exodus 24:3

In the first five books ascribed to Moses, the Pentateuch, or Torah as it is known in the Jewish tradition, are found a complex code of liturgical legislation. There are laws on the various types of sacrifice, on the installation of priests, and on purity and impurity.

Perhaps the most notable laws have to do with dietary restrictions. Following these restrictions today is referred to as keeping kosher.

Animals That Can Be Eaten

Whatsoever parteth the hoof, and is cloven-footed, and cheweth the cud, among the beasts, that shall ye eat.

– Leviticus 11:3

This includes cows, goats, deer – all animals with cloven hooves that chew their cud.

Notwithstanding, thou mayest kill and eat flesh in all thy gates, whatsoever thy soul lustest after, according to the blessing of the Lord thy God which he hath given thee: the unclean and the clean may eat thereof, as of the roebuck, and as of the hart.

– Deuteronomy 12:15

These are the beasts ye shall eat: the ox, the sheep, and the goat, the hart, and the roebuck, and the fallow deer, and the wild goat, and the pygarg, and the wild ox, and the chamois. And every beast that parteth the hoof, and cleaveth the cleft into two claws, and cheweth the cud among the beasts, that ye shall eat.

– Deuteronomy 14:4-6

These shall ye eat of all that are in the waters: whatsoever hath fins and scales in the waters, in the seas, and in the rivers, them shall ye eat.

– Leviticus 11:9

Even these of them ye may eat; the locust after his kind, and the bald locust after his kind, and the beetle after his kind, and the grasshopper after his kind. But all other flying creeping things, which have four feet, shall be an abomination unto you.

– Leviticus 11:22-23

Animals That Cannot Be Eaten

These shall ye not eat of them that chew the cud, or of them that divide the hoof: as the camel, because he cheweth the cud, but divideth not the hoof...

– Leviticus 11:4

The list specifically prohibits the camel, coney (what we would call a rabbit), hare and swine.

Nevertheless these ye shall not eat of them that chew the cud, or of them that divide the cloven hoof; as the camel, and the hare, and the coney: for they chew the cud, but divide not the hoof; therefore they are unclean unto you. And the swine, because it divideth the hoof, yet cheweth the cud, it is unclean unto you: ye shall not eat of their flesh, nor touch their dead carcass."

– Deuteronomy 14:7-8

And all that have not fins and scales in the seas, and in the rivers, of all that move in the waters, and of any living thing which is in the waters, they shall be an abomination unto you.

— Leviticus 11:10

And these are they which ye shall have in abomination among the fowls; they shall not be eaten, they are an abomination: the eagle, and the ossifrage, and the osprey, and the vulture, and the kite after his kind; every raven after his kind; and the owl, and the night hawk, and the cuckoo, and the hawk after his kind, and the little owl, and the cormorant, and the great owl, and the swan, and the pelican, and the gier eagle, and the stork, the heron after her kind, and the lapwing, and the bat. All fowls that creep, going upon all four, shall be an abomination unto you.

— Leviticus 11:13-20

And every creeping thing that creepeth upon the earth shall be an abomination; it shall not be eaten. Whatsoever goeth upon the belly, and whatsoever goeth upon all four, or whatsoever hath more feet among all creeping things that creep upon the earth, them ye shall not eat; for they are an abomination. Ye shall not make yourselves abominable with any creeping thing that creepeth, neither shall ye make yourselves unclean with them, that ye should be defiled thereby.

— Leviticus 11:41-43

And ye shall be holy men unto me: neither shall ye eat any flesh that is torn of beasts in the field; ye shall cast it to the dogs.

— Exodus 22:31

Ye shall eat no manner of fat, of ox, or of sheep, or of goat. And the fat of the beast that dieth of it-

self, and the fat of that which is torn with beasts, may be used in any other use: but ye shall in no wise eat of it. For whosoever eateth the fat of the beast, of which men offer an offering made by fire unto the Lord, even the soul that eateth it shall be cut off from his people."

– Leviticus 7:23-25

Moreover ye shall eat no manner of blood, whether it be of fowl or of beast, in any of your dwellings. Whatsoever soul it be that eateth any manner of blood, even that soul shall be cut off from his people.

– Leviticus 7:26-27

Why did God permit us to eat certain foods, but not others? Many people try to find the justifications behind these laws. For example, they say that we were forbidden to eat pork because it could carry trichinosis if not properly cooked. However, these people tend to miss the point. Part of the covenant God set up with the Hebrews when they accepted the role as Chosen People was to follow God's rules. As creator of the world and all that exists within it, God has the right to set up laws and forbid us to do things, regardless of whether or not we understand those rules.

New Testament Laws

The New Testament is the story of Jesus and how he died for our sins. Because of his own sacrifice, we no longer are required to make sacrifices of animal flesh.

In Paul's letter to the Romans it is written:

I know, and am persuaded by the Lord Jesus, that there is nothing unclean of itself: but to him that esteemeth any thing to be unclean, to him it is unclean. But if thy brother be grieved with thy meat, now walkest thou not charitably. Destroy not him with thy meat, for whom Christ died. Let not then your good be evil spoken of: For the kingdom of God is not meat and drink; but righteousness, and peace, and joy in the Holy Ghost. For he that in these things serveth Christ is acceptable to God, and approved of men. For meat destroy not the work of God. All things indeed are pure; but it is evil for that man who eateth with offence. It is good neither to eat flesh, nor to drink wine, nor any thing whereby thy brother stumbleth, or is offended, or is made weak.

– Romans 14:14-21

I look at this passage as "When in Rome, eat as the Romans do." Here, Paul teaches that there is nothing unclean except by our perception. We are now allowed to eat anything. However, we should keep in mind the perceptions and feelings of those around us. In other words, if eating pork offends your host or neighbors, refrain from doing so. Likewise, if you are given something you may not like, eat it anyway so you don't offend those who have shared their meal with you. Jesus himself teaches this when he sends out the 70 appointees to speak in his name. He instructs them that "into whatsoever city ye enter, and they receive you, eat such things as are set before you."

Prayers of Thanksgiving

When thou has eaten and art full, then thou shalt bless the Lord thy God for the good land which he hath given thee.
— Deuteronomy 8:10

Whatever you eat, remember to give thanks for the food set before you. Here are some common table graces from around the world.

Hebrew Prayers of Thanksgiving

Though our mouths were full of song as the sea, and our tongues of exultation as the multitude of its waves, and our lips of praise as the wide-extended firmament; though our eyes shone with light like the sun and the moon, and our hands were spread forth like the eagles of heaven, and our feet were swift as hinds, we should still be unable to thank thee and bless thy name, O Lord our God and God of our fathers, for one thousandth or one ten thousandth part of the bounties which thou has bestowed upon our fathers and upon us. Amen.

✿ ✿ ✿ ✿ ✿ ✿ ✿

Blessed are You, O Lord our God, Eternal King. You feed the whole world with Your goodness, with grace, with loving kindness, and with tender mercy. You give food to all flesh, for Your loving kindness endures forever. Through Your great goodness, food has never failed us. May it not fail us forever, for Your name's sake, since You nourish and sustain all living things, and do good to all, and provide food for all Your creatures whom

14

You have created. Blessed are You, O Lord, Who gives food to all. Amen.

✤ ✤ ✤ ✤ ✤ ✤ ✤

The eyes of all wait upon thee; and thou givest them their meat in due season. Amen.

– Psalm 145:15

Christian Prayers of Thanksgiving

We come to join in the banquet of love. Let it open our hearts and break down the fears that keep us from loving one another. Amen.

– Dominican Prayer

✤ ✤ ✤ ✤ ✤ ✤ ✤

Some hae meat and canna eat,
And some wad eat that want it;
But we hae meat and we can eat,
And sae the Lord be thankit. Amen.

– Robert Burns

✤ ✤ ✤ ✤ ✤ ✤ ✤

Be present at our table, Lord.
Be here and everywhere adored.
Thy creatures bless and grant that we
May feast in paradise with Thee. Amen.

– John Cennick

✤ ✤ ✤ ✤ ✤ ✤ ✤

Thank you Heavenly Father for the blue
    skies above me,
The green grass below me, and
    the good friends beside me.
Thank you Heavenly Father for the good
    food in front of me.
May peace reign over the world. Amen.

✤ ✤ ✤ ✤ ✤ ✤ ✤

This food, which you have already blessed in the
  giving,
So further bless in our partaking. Amen.

✤ ✤ ✤ ✤ ✤ ✤ ✤

God is great, and God is good,
And we thank him for our food;
By his hand we all are fed;
Give us Lord our daily bread. Amen.

✤ ✤ ✤ ✤ ✤ ✤ ✤

May the peace and blessing of the Lord
Descend upon us as we receive of his bounty,
And may our hearts be filled with love for
  one another. Amen.

✤ ✤ ✤ ✤ ✤ ✤ ✤

For health and food; for
  love and friends,
For everything thy
  goodness sends,
Father, in heaven, we
  thank thee.
Dear Heavenly Father,
We give thanks
  for the pleasure
Of gathering together for
  this occasion.

We give thanks for this
  food prepared by loving hands.
We give thanks for life, for freedom, and the
  ability to enjoy it all and all other blessings.
Amen.

✤ ✤ ✤ ✤ ✤ ✤ ✤

We thank you, Lord, for happy hearts,
For rain and sunny weather;
We thank you for the food we eat,

And that we are together.
Gracious Father, Bless this food,
For Thy glory and Thy good. Amen.

✤ ✤ ✤ ✤ ✤ ✤ ✤

As we partake of this food we pray for health and
strength to carry on and try to live as You would
have us. This we ask in the name of Christ, Your
Heavenly Son. Amen.

✤ ✤ ✤ ✤ ✤ ✤ ✤

Heavenly Father, we thank Thee for this food,
For health and strength and all things good.
May others all these blessings share,
And hearts be grateful everywhere. Amen.

✤ ✤ ✤ ✤ ✤ ✤ ✤

To God who gives us daily bread,
A thankful song we raise,
And pray that He who sends us food
Will fill our hearts with praise. Amen.

✤ ✤ ✤ ✤ ✤ ✤ ✤

Bless us, O Lord, for these our gifts that we are
about to receive from your bounty through Christ
our Lord. Amen.

✤ ✤ ✤ ✤ ✤ ✤ ✤

For each new morning with its light,
For rest and shelter of the night,
For health and food, for love and friends,
For everything Thy goodness sends. Amen.

– Ralph Waldo Emerson

✤ ✤ ✤ ✤ ✤ ✤ ✤

Father, we thank Thee for this food,
For health and strength and all things good.
May others all these blessings share,
And hearts be grateful everywhere. Amen.

Orthodox Christian Breakfast Prayer

O Most Holy Trinity, have mercy on us! Lord, cleanse us from our sins! Master, pardon our transgressions! Holy One, visit and heal our infirmities for Thy name's sake. Glory be to the Father, and to the Son, and to the Holy Spirit, now and ever and unto ages of ages. Amen.

Lord, have mercy! (3 times)

O Christ God, bless the food and drink of Thy servants, for Thou art holy, always, now and ever and unto ages of ages. Amen.

Orthodox Christian Supper Prayer

The poor shall eat and be satisfied, and those who seek the Lord shall praise Him; their hearts shall live forever! Glory be to the Father, and to the Son, and to the Holy Spirit, now and ever and unto ages of ages. Amen.

Lord, have mercy! (3 times)

O Christ God, bless the food and drink of Thy servants, for Thou art holy, always, now and ever and unto ages of ages. Amen.

Muslim Prayers of Thanksgiving

The word *Islam*, or *Al Islam* in Arabic, means submission and peace. Islam is a monotheistic religion based on a belief in Allah, the God Who is One. Islam shares a common history with both Christianity and Judaism, and reveres among its prophets Abraham, Moses and Jesus Christ.

In the name of Allah, the Lord of all Beings,
the Compassionate and Merciful,
the Sustainer of the World,

the Master of the Day of Judgment,
You alone do we worship, and to You alone we
　pray.
Guide us on the straightforward path, the path of
　those whom You have blessed.
Keep us from the path of those who have brought
　Your wrath,
and from those who wander astray. Amen.

Native American Grace

This prayer was given to me several years ago, and
I'm unsure which tribe originated it. I feel the words
are a beautiful tribute to the bounty of the earth and
wish to share them here.

We give thanks to our mother, the earth, who
sustains us. We give thanks to the rivers and
streams which supply us with water. We give
thanks to all herbs, which furnish medicines for
the cure of our diseases. We give thanks to the
corn, and to her sisters, the beans and squash,
which give us life. We give thanks to the bushes
and trees, which provide us with fruit. We give
thanks to the wind, which, moving the air, has
banished diseases. We give thanks to the moon
and the stars, which have given us their light
when the sun was gone. We give thanks to our
grandfather He-no, that he has protected his
grandchildren from witches and reptiles, and has
given to us his rain. We give thanks to the sun,
that he has looked upon the earth with a benefi-
cent eye. Lastly, we give thanks to the Great
Spirit, in whom is embodied all goodness, and
who directs all things for the good of his children.
Amen.

The Foods

Juices and Teas

I would lead thee, and bring thee into my mother's house, who would instruct me: I would cause thee to drink of spiced wine of the juice of my pomegranate.
— Song of Solomon 8:2

The pomegranate is a fruit native to the Middle East that has been cultivated for thousands of years. When Moses and the children of Israel lived in the wilderness, they dearly missed the pomegranates of Egypt. King Solomon had an entire orchard of pomegranate trees, and the pillars of his temple were decorated with carvings of lilies and pomegranates. Pomegranates grew in abundance in Galilee, so Jesus would no doubt have eaten them. The prophet Muhammad instructed everyone to "eat the pomegranate, for it purges the system of envy and hatred."

Our word pomegranate is derived from Old French *pome garnete*, which literally means "seeded apple," although the fruit has no relation to the apple. In the Middle East it was called *rimmon*. According to legend, there are 613 seeds in each pomegranate, one for each of the mitzvahs, or good deeds, of Hebrew tradition. The fruit is roughly the size of an orange and has a smooth, leathery skin that ranges from yellow to red. Its flesh has many tiny chambers filled with seeds and juicy pulp. Pomegranates are usually eaten fresh. The juice is the source of grenadine, often used in baking and mixed drinks.

The following recipe calls for pomegranate juice. You can buy it at Middle Eastern groceries and some gourmet shops or make it yourself from fresh pomegranates. Pomegranates are available in many local groceries, especially in the fall. You can use an ordinary orange juice squeezer to extract the pomegranate juice. The ancients would have warmed the fruit between their hands, rolling it back and forth, to soften the pulp. They would then cut a hole in the rind and squeeze out the juice.

Sweetened Pomegranate Juice

3 cups fresh pomegranate juice
½ cup lemon juice
Pinch of sugar or 1 tsp warmed honey
Dash of salt
Water to adjust strength

Combine all ingredients, serve cold over ice. Serves 2.

Note: Some recipes call for orange blossom water. If you'd like to try it, add 1 Tbs at a time until you reach the desired taste. You may also try seltzer water instead of regular water.

Mint, Hibiscus and Hyssop Tea

When I traveled through the Middle East a few years back, I was served tea wherever I went – usually mint or hibiscus. Once when I had a bit of a cold I was served hyssop tea. In Cairo, I met a family of Coptic Christians, direct descendants of the ancient Egyptians, who served me a wonderfully refreshing mint tea that I still dream about. Most people grow their own mint, just as their ancient ancestors did, but purchase tea bags like their western counterparts. Believe it or not, the most common tea I saw in Egypt was good old Lipton!

Some biblical scholars say that mint is one of the bitter herbs mentioned in Exodus. It was probably the variety *Mentha longifolia*, because that is the one most extensively cultivated in the Middle East today. Although there are many varieties, in cooking mint usually refers to spearmint or peppermint. I personally think spearmint makes a better tea, but that's just one woman's opinion.

Mint Tea

8 tsp sugar, or honey to taste
1 Tbs fresh mint leaves
5 cups boiling water
4 tea bags
Wedges of lemon

Steep sugar, tea bags and mint leaves in boiling water. Serve with lemon wedges in a glass. Serves 4.

Note: Green tea provides a more delicate flavor.

Herbal Mint Tea

½ cup mint
Large pinch saffron
Sugar to taste
3 cups boiling water.

Combine all ingredients and let steep several minutes. Serves 2.

HIBISCUS tea, known as *karkady*, is one of the most popular drinks in the Middle East. Made from the dark red petals of the hibiscus flower, it is served in almost every café, hotel and shop. When bargaining with merchants, it is not unusual to negotiate over a glass or two of this delicious tea. Even a simple transaction can take an hour because of the socializing. When I came home from my first trip, I had packets of the dried petals tucked into every nook and cranny of my backpack.

Hibiscus Tea

1 cup dried hibiscus petals
6 cups water
Sugar or honey to taste

Soak hibiscus petals in cold water overnight. Bring to a boil and immediately remove from heat. Strain, discard the petals, and sweeten with sugar or honey to taste. Serve hot or cold. Serves 3.

Variation: Lime juice is sometimes added to provide tang. If you wish to try it, add 1/2 cup lime juice for every six cups water.

Hyssop Tea

1 cup wildflower honey
¼ cup water
½ cup fresh hyssop flowers (or 3 Tbs dried)
½ tsp anise seed, crushed (optional)

Warm the honey over medium heat and slowly stir in the water until blended. Bring to a boil and add the hyssop and anise seed. Reduce heat and let simmer 20 minutes. This produces a syrup that can be taken as a cough remedy or reconstituted with hot water for a tea.

Note: Some herbalists recommend making a strong tea of hyssop leaves and applying it as a poultice to speed the healing of bruises. The leaves are also used in internal cough remedies.

Beer

You are the one who hold with both hands the great sweet wort, Brewing it with honey and wine.
— Hymn to Ninkasi, 1800 B.C.

A while back, a friend forwarded me a letter from an organization called the Beer Church. It claimed Jesus did not change water into wine – but beer! The idea, I thought, was ludicrous. While there are countless references to wine and winemaking, I could not recall any mention of the disciples visiting alehouses. I needed more proof.

One trip to the library later, I had learned how, during the days of Jesus, Egypt was a major exporter of beer to the entire Mediterranean region. Beer had been drunk for thousands of years before the birth of Christ. There was even an early Sumerian beer goddess named Ninkasi.

Some scholars believe that beer came before bread with the accidental discovery of barley fermentation. They also believe that alcohol was the real motivation behind the agricultural revolution when hunter-gathers settled in farms.

In biblical times, grain was the principle crop for the region, not grapes, which would make beer more common. As such, beer was the drink of the common folk, while wine was enjoyed by the elite – much as it is in

25

our own society. Furthermore, the original texts of the Bible say that Jesus changed water into a "strong drink" but do not specifically mention what that drink is. Since Jesus rubbed elbows with the poor and needy and not the elite, it is possible he would serve them beer, their drink of choice.

What do you think?

Biblical Era Beer

In the ancient world, beer was used as medicine, in ritual and as a beverage. Preserved on several clay tablets is the Hymn to Ninkasi, which has a recipe for beer that is nearly 4,000 years old! It calls for mixing *bappir*, a type of bread, with water and "aromatics" and setting it to ferment in large vats before being strained.

Everyone drank beer – men, women, even children. Beer was so important in ancient society, that the Code of Hammurabi said tavern owners who overcharged their customers could be put to death by drowning!

Two major breweries, Anchor Brewing Co. of San Francisco and Newcastle of Great Britain, have experimented with making a modern version of Ninkasi's brew.

Wine

*When thou comest into
thy neighbour's
vineyard, then thou
mayest eat grapes
thy fill at thine own
pleasure; but thou
shalt not put any
in thy vessel.*
– Deuteronomy 23:24

Lamech, Noah's son, had said his
father would "bring us relief and com-
fort from our work and the toil of our
hands." After the great flood, one of the
first things Noah did was to plant his wine
grapes and start a new industry, "And Noah began to
be an husbandman, and he planted a vineyard: and he
drank of the wine, and was drunken." (Genesis 9:20-21)
With the first wine, comes the first case of drunkenness and, no doubt, the first hangover.

According to archaeological records, grapes probably
came from Iran and spread south and west. Clay vessels with wine residue dating to roughly 5,000 B.C.
have been found in the Zagros Mountains of northern
Iran. Grapes are mentioned in the Sumerian poem the
Epic of Gilgamesh which was written around 3,000
B.C. Grape harvesting and winemaking are depicted in
ancient Egyptian paintings.

Wine was well-known – and probably well-loved –
throughout the ancient world.

The Bible does permit and in some cases encourages
the use of alcohol. Jesus turned water into wine at a wed-

ding banquet and was known to drink it himself. "The Son of man came eating and drinking, and they say, Behold a man gluttonous and a winebibber, a friend of publicans and sinners. But wisdom is justified of her children." (Matthew 11:19).

Paul said to his disciple Timothy, "Drink no longer water, but use a little wine for thy stomach's sake and thine often infirmities."

Wine was used sacramentally, medicinally, and as a beverage with meals. "And he took the cup, and when he had given thanks, he gave it to them: and they all drank of it." (Mark 14:23)

There is nothing wrong with drinking alcohol in moderation. What the Bible does condemn is drunkenness and drinking to excess. "Let us walk honestly, as in the day; not in rioting and drunkenness, not in chambering and wantonness, not in strife and envying." (Romans 13:13)

So feel free to have a glass or two of wine with dinner, as long as you know your own limits.

Bible Method for Making Wine

Wine appears many times in the Bible. Grapes were picked by hand and carried in baskets (Jeremiah 6:9) to the wine press, a shallow vat-like excavation carved in rock (Isaiah 5:2). Once there, the grapes were crushed by stomping on them (Job 24:11), often to the accompaniment of work songs (Jeremiah 25:30). It was a vigorous task and people's clothes were often stained by the juice (Isaiah 63:1-3). New wine, partially fermented, was put into skin flasks or stone jars to finish its fermentation (Job 32:19). Old wine, fully fermented, was stored away (Luke 5:39).

In the ancient world, wine was often spiced for two

reasons – because it tasted good and because certain herbs could mask the taste of poor quality wine.

You may try spicing wine yourself by combining the following ingredients:

**1 bottle dry white wine or
1 bottle rosé or red wine**

**3-4 sprigs of herb (try mint, rose petals, or
whatever strikes your fancy)**

In a non-metallic container, steep the herbs in the wine and set in a cool, dark place overnight. Some herbs, such as rose petals, may actually need several weeks to take on the right flavor. If so, place the wine in sterilized jars and seal. Filter before serving. Serves 6.

Milk

*And I am come down to deliver them
out of the hand of the Egyptians, and to
bring them up out of that land unto a
good land and a large, unto a land
flowing with milk and honey...*
– Exodus 3:8

Milk has sometimes been called the perfect food because it provides many necessary nutrients, such as protein and vitamin D. Today, most of the milk consumed in America comes from cows. In the Middle East and parts of Southern Europe, milk from sheep, water buffalo and even camels is used, but goat's milk is still the preferred variety, much as it was in the ancient world.

In biblical times, milk was made into butter, cheese and *leben*, a type of watery yogurt. Milk was not usually consumed as a beverage beyond childhood, as indicated in Hebrews 5:12-13, "Ye...are in need of milk, and not of strong meat. For every one that useth milk is unskillful in the word of righteousness, for he is a babe." This might be, in part, due to the difficult task of keeping milk fresh in those days. Milk could be preserved for short periods by lacing it with spices, often mint or other savories. The boiling process also killed a number of microorganisms found in the milk.

Baby's Milk

Goat's milk – still the preferred variety in the Middle East – can be diluted with distilled water to make a baby formula that, some researchers say, is more nutritious and easier to digest than man-made formulas. It was probably what was once fed to babies whose mothers could not breast-feed. However, you should first speak with your pediatrician before deciding to give your young child milk. Many doctors will caution against milk consumption for children under 1 year.

While touring the Middle East, I was often served *sahalab* at breakfast. It is quite delicious and reminds me a bit of *chai* — the spiced tea. You will need sahalab powder, which can be found in some larger supermarkets and spice shops, as well as Middle Eastern, Indian and international grocery stores. Pistachios, also found in the recipe, are one of two nuts mentioned in the Old Testament. They are said to have grown in the Hanging Gardens of Babylon.

Sahalab Milk

    1 tsp sahalab powder
    1 cup milk
    Honey or sugar to taste
    Few drops vanilla
    Dash of cinnamon
    1 tsp pistachio nuts, crushed fine

Stir the sahalab with a little of the cold milk to form a paste. Slowly bring the remaining milk to a boil, being careful not to let it scorch. Mix in the sahalab and add sweetener. Reduce heat and let simmer a few minutes. Stir in vanilla. Serve hot with a dash of cinnamon and crushed pistachio nuts on top. Serves 1.

Cheese and Yogurt

(Shobi) brought honey, and butter, and sheep, and cheese of kine for David, and for the people that were with him.
– 2 Samuel 17:29

Archaeologists have discovered that cheese was made at least 8,000 years ago from cow's and goat's milk and stored in tall clay jars. Egyptian wall paintings depict workers making both butter and cheese and show milk stored in bags made of animal skin.

For easy transport, nomadic tribes would carry skin bags strapped on a pack animal's back. Fermentation would take place in the bags, causing milk to curdle. The constant motion of the animals would break up the cheese into curds while the remaining liquid, the whey, would provide a refreshing drink. Salt could be added to the curds to provide a bit of savory flavor.

THE following recipe is for a very simple egg cheese. The vanilla is a modern addition – the ancients might have used a variety of herbs and spices to flavor cheese.

Simple Egg Cheese

    1½ qts whole milk
    1 dozen eggs, beaten
    2 tsp vanilla
    1 Tbs sugar
    ¼ tsp salt

Heat the milk to almost boiling, being careful not to scorch it. Reduce heat and add eggs, vanilla, sugar and salt, beating thoroughly. Continue to cook over low heat, stirring gently, until mixture curdles. Remove from heat and set aside for half an hour or so to let some of the whey separate. Use a slotted spoon to transfer curds to a colander lined with cheesecloth. Tie the ends of the cheesecloth together with string and hang it over a bucket overnight so that the whey drips out. Refrigerate before removing from cheesecloth. Slice into servings. You can also brush the finished cheese with egg yolk and bake in a low oven until lightly browned. Makes 2 small cheeses.

Note: My friend Kirsten uses clean knee-high stockings instead of cheesecloth. She says they work better than cheesecloth, and you can easily tie the end.

FOR the following recipe, you will need to use natural yogurt because varieties with pectin or other additives will not work.

Yogurt Cheese

5 cups natural yogurt
Pinch salt, or to taste

Scoop yogurt into a cheesecloth-lined sieve and place over a bowl. Blend in a pinch of salt. Set in refrigerator for 24 hours until liquid drains away. Discard liquid – you should have about 2 cups of yogurt cheese left. Great when served with fruit or spread on pita bread. Serves 4.

IN PARTS of Turkey and Armenia there are many centenarians – people who live to be over 100. They credit their healthy, active lives to a diet rich in yogurt. In rural areas throughout the Middle East, yogurt is still made the old-fashioned way. Milk is boiled in uncovered pans to sterilize it and evaporate some of the water. When cool, a spoonful or two of yogurt from a previous batch is blended into the mixture to act as a starter. By the next day, the yogurt is ready to eat.

This dish is known in the Middle East as *mast o khiar*. It features cucumbers which originated in India and quickly spread throughout the Middle East and Europe.

Yogurt with Cucumbers

1 cucumber, peeled and chopped
1 16-oz container of
  plain yogurt
1 tsp garlic
½ tsp dillweed, minced fine
Salt and pepper to taste

Blend all ingredients, chill before serving. Excellent as a side dish or alone. Serves 4.

Note: For a cooler variety, omit the dillweed and add 3 Tbs of chopped fresh mint.

Butter

Surely the churning of milk bringeth
forth butter... so the forcing of
wrath bringeth forth strife.
— Proverbs 30:33

Clarified butter, known as *samneh*, can be kept for long periods of time without turning rancid. In Egypt and Israel, it is sold in large tubs, but in the U.S., it's easier to make your own. Melt one pound of butter in a heavy skillet over very low heat. Simmer 35-40 minutes until a foam forms on the surface and butter is light golden brown. Skim off foam and strain butter through cheesecloth. Store in the refrigerator or any cool place.

Spiced Butter

- 2 lbs butter, cut into cubes
- 1 yellow onion, peeled and chopped
- 3½ Tbs minced garlic
- 1 Tbs fresh ginger, chopped fine
- 2 tsp turmeric
- ½ tsp ground cardamom
- ½ tsp cinnamon
- Dash of nutmeg
- Dash of ground cloves

Melt butter in a heavy cast-iron pan over medium heat. Do not let it scorch. Stir in all remaining ingredients. Reduce heat and simmer, uncovered, for 30 minutes. Do not stir! Solids will sink to the bottom of the pan. Carefully pour the liquid into clean sterilized jars, using cheesecloth to strain away the solids. Let cool and refrigerate.

Eggs

*Is there any taste in the
white of an egg?
— Job 6:6*

In the 9th century, the Church banned the eating of
eggs during Lent. Of course, the ducks and hens were
unaware of the ban so they would keep on laying. The
eggs were collected and saved until Easter, often elab-
orately decorated. On Easter Sunday they would be made
into huge omelettes and enjoyed by the entire household.

This recipe for eggs with pine nut sauce is an up-
dated version of an ancient Middle Eastern recipe.

Eggs with Pine Nut Sauce
   2 oz pine nuts
   4 Tbs red wine vinegar
   2 tsp honey
   Pinch of dried pepper
   6 hard-boiled eggs

Soak the pine nuts in vinegar overnight. Combine
pine nuts, vinegar, honey and pepper in a blender or
food processor. Slice the eggs and serve with the sauce.
Serves 2.

Middle Eastern Scrambled Eggs
   2 Tbs butter
   ½ tsp minced garlic
   6 eggs
   Salt to taste
   2-3 Tbs white vinegar

Melt butter in frying pan and sauté garlic. Beat eggs and season to taste. Carefully pour egg mixture into the frying pan, stirring continuously. Whisk in vinegar 1 Tbs at a time. (It's not very traditional, but I prefer champagne vinegar for my eggs.) Your eggs will have a rich and creamy texture. Serves 2.

I always thought this was an Eastern European dish because my Polish grandmother used to make it at Easter time when I was little. The eggs take on a lovely orange-brown hue that we always preferred to the pastel color egg kits. I've since learned this dish is quite ancient, and of Middle Eastern origin, where it is still a favorite appetizer.

Onion Skin Eggs
1 dozen eggs
Skins from 3 large yellow onions
Water to cover

Place eggs and onion skins in a large cooking pot and cover with water. Simmer on very, very low heat for 6 to 8 hours. Add more water if necessary. You may even pour a tablespoon of olive oil on the surface to prevent the water from evaporating as quickly. The eggs come out very creamy. Serves 4.

Fruits and Vegetables

God said, Behold, I have given you
every herb bearing seed, which is upon
the face of all the earth, and every tree,
in which is the fruit of a tree yielding
seed; to you it shall be for meat.
— Genesis 1:29

Although God also gives Adam "dominion over the fish of the sea, and over the fowl of the air, and over every living thing that moveth upon the earth" (Genesis 1:28), he does not instruct that they should be eaten. What God does say is that he has given to these creatures "every green herb for meat." In the Garden of Eden, man and beast lived in harmony, and even our fellow creatures did not devour one another.

It was not until after the flood, when the Ark came to rest and God blessed Noah, that we were told we could eat meat as well. "Every moving thing that liveth shall be meat for you; even as the green herb have I given you all things." (Genesis 9:3)

Even so, most people of the biblical era remained vegetarians – at least the common folk did. Kings, merchants and others who could afford to eat meat did so, but for most people, vegetables, legumes and grains remained the staple of their diet. Even today, while the average American consumes more than 200 pounds of meat in a year, the average Middle Eastern native eats only 12-15 pounds.

There is a branch of scholarship that claims both Daniel and Jesus were vegetarians. When Daniel was imprisoned by Babylonian King Nebuchadnezzar, he "would not defile himself with the portion of the king's meat, nor with the wine which he drank; therefore he requested of the prince of the eunuchs that he might not defile himself." (Daniel 1:8) Instead he asked for pulse (legumes) and water.

Jesus may have been a member of the Nazarene Essenes, a Jewish sect that followed a vegetarian diet and condemned animal sacrifice. Epiphanus, a 4th century church elder, said "They who believed in Christ were called Essenes before they were called Christians." In Isaiah 7:14-15, it was proclaimed that "a virgin shall conceive, and bear a son, and shall call his name Immanuel. Butter and honey shall he eat, so that he may know to refuse the evil, and choose the good."

There was a belief that meat, like alcohol – both of which were permitted by God – corrupted the soul unless avoided or taken in moderation. "It is good neither to eat flesh, nor to drink wine, nor anything whereby thy brother stumbleth, or is offended, or is made weak." (Romans 14:21) It was prophesied that the Messiah would eat only butter and honey so that his heart would remain pure.

Critics of this theory point out that the King James version of the New Testament has several passages that say Jesus ate meat. However, the words being translated here are

Greek – *trophe* and *broma*. They mean food but not any particular type of food. The Greek word for meat, *kareas*, is never used in connection with Jesus.

The same critics bring up the story of the loaves and fishes. If Jesus were a vegetarian, did he make an exception and eat fish? The word translated as fish may mean fishweed, a popular type of dried seaweed that is still eaten by Palestinians today. Matthew says that Jesus arrived at this place by boat. If the crowd wanted to eat fish, wouldn't it have been readily accessible along the coast? Many of the disciples were former fishermen, but nobody ever mentioned going fishing.

These arguments can go round and round, with other scholars pointing out that Jesus ate fish after his resurrection: "And they gave him a piece of a broiled fish, and of an honeycomb. And he took it, and did eat before them." (Luke 24:42-43) There are many vegetarians who abstain from meat but eat fish. They are known as "pesco-vegetarians." If Jesus were a vegetarian, he may have adhered to such a diet. Some Catholics still observe meatless Fridays when they substitute fish for the main course.

If you are interested in learning more about this argument, visit **www.jesusveg.com**, hosted by PETA (People for the Ethical Treatment of Animals). You can also try **www.a1.nu/christian/vegetarian/** where you will find links to several essays on biblical vegetarianism.

Carrots with Cardamom

2 cups milk
1 lb carrots, peeled and grated
1 cup sugar
½ tsp cardamom
1 Tbs grated lemon zest
2 Tbs butter, melted
2 Tbs flour
Pistachios and raisins

Bring milk to a near boil. Reduce heat and add carrots, sugar, cardamom and lemon zest. Simmer until carrots are tender. Drain in a colander, pressing down on carrots to remove as much juice as possible. Set liquid aside. Whisk butter and flour together to form a roux. Add carrots, tossing to coat with butter mixture. Pour the cooking liquid over the carrots and continue to cook for another five minutes, stirring occasionally. Serve hot with a garnish of pistachios and raisins. Serves 4.

And the daughter of Zion is left as a cottage in a vineyard, as a lodge in a garden of cucumbers, as a besieged city.
— Isaiah 1:8

CULINARY scholars say that two types of cucumber grew during biblical times. One variety, *cucumis sativas*, originated in India and had a smooth white skin. The other was green, long and thin.

Nowadays, cucumbers are found in cosmetic preparations and slices of the fruit are used as a pick-me-up for tired eyes. The ancients also used cucumbers in cosmetics and medicines. A lotion made by boiling cucumber slices with rose or quince petals would freshen the complexion.

This recipe from Israel calls for feta cheese, a semi-soft tangy cheese cured in brine. Feta is said to have originated in ancient Greece. In Homer's *Odyssey*, Polyphemus the Cyclops makes a cheese from sheep's milk.

Cheese and Cucumber Salad

½ lb feta cheese
2 Tbs lemon juice
2 Tbs olive oil
1 large sweet onion, peeled and chopped fine
1 cucumber, peeled and diced
Salt and pepper to taste

Combine the feta cheese, lemon juice and olive oil with a fork. Add the onion and cucumber; season to taste with salt and pepper. This salad is best served with bread. Serves 4.

Cucumber Salad

1 cucumber, peeled and diced
1 large tomato
1 small onion, chopped fine
1 Tbs fresh mint or parsley, minced
1 Tbs olive oil
1 Tbs lemon juice or vinegar
1 tsp minced garlic
Salt and pepper to taste

Combine all ingredients. Chill before serving. Serves 2.

EGGPLANT is native to southern and eastern Asia, where it has been cultivated since antiquity. It's extremely popular in Middle Eastern and Mediterranean cuisine. The large, egg-shaped fruit can vary in color from deep purple or red to yellow or white. It is the white coloring that gives it its popular name.

This salad is delicious as a dip, a spread or a side dish.

Eggplant Salad

1 large eggplant
1 medium sweet onion, peeled and chopped
3 Tbs lemon juice
1 Tbs olive oil
1 Tbs minced garlic
½ tsp salt, or to taste
¼ tsp pepper, or to taste
¼ tsp cumin
Dash of chili pepper

Roast eggplant at 350°F for 1 hour. Peel and run through a food processor with all other ingredients. Serves 4.

We remember the fish which we did
eat in Egypt freely; the cucumbers,
and the melons, and the leeks, and the
onions, and the garlick.
— Numbers 11:5

ONIONS are one of the world's oldest cultivated plants. Although hailed as a cure-all and enjoyed as a side dish for more than 6,000 years, there is only one mention of them in the Bible – but it was remembered with longing by the exiled people when they left Egypt. The Egyptians, who regarded the onion as a symbol of the universe, fed them to the slaves who worked on the pyramids – many of whom were Israelites. Today, onions are still praised for their curative properties.

Stuffed Onions

> 3 large sweet onions
> Water for boiling
> 4 Tbs pomegranate syrup (available at Middle Eastern groceries)
> 2 Tbs sugar
> 1 cup boiling water
> 3 Tbs vegetable oil

FOR THE STUFFING:

> 2 lbs ground beef or lamb
> 1 Tbs cinnamon
> ¾ cup fresh mint, chopped fine
> Salt and pepper to taste
> ½ cup parsley, chopped fine

Peel the onions and slice off the ends. Make a slice from the top of each onion toward the center. Cook onions in lightly salted, boiling water for about 15 minutes or until the layers of the onion begin to open. Drain. When cool, carefully separate the layers.

Combine all of the stuffing ingredients – you'll achieve the best mixture by kneading with your hands. Place a heaping spoonful of the meat in each onion layer and roll up. Place the onion rolls in a large, cast-iron frying pan.

Dissolve the pomegranate syrup and sugar in the boiling water. Stir in the oil and pour the entire mixture over the onion rolls. If needed, add additional water to cover the onion rolls. To prevent them from floating, place a weight – either a plate or a pot lid that is slightly too small for the pot – on top.

Simmer over medium heat for half an hour. The onions are done when they are tender and have soaked up the water. You can serve them as is, but they will look more appealing if you place them in an oven-proof dish and broil them for several minutes.

If desired, you can sprinkle more sugar on the surface before broiling. Best when hot but can also be eaten cold. Serves 3 to 6.

ALTHOUGH it is not much used anymore, purslane grows wild in Israel just as it did in biblical times. You can sometimes find it at your local grocery. Young leaves can be used in a salad and are particularly enhanced by citrus flavors. If purslane is not available in your area, substitute dandelion greens or spinach.

Purslane

1 lb purslane greens
3 Tbs vinegar or lemon juice
½ tsp mustard
¼ cup olive oil
Salt and pepper to taste

Lightly steam the purslane and pat dry. Combine the

vinegar, mustard, olive oil, salt and pepper. Pour over the greens and toss. Serve immediately. Serves 4.

TOMATOES were unknown in the ancient world, but they're a common ingredient in today's Middle Eastern cooking. If you'd rather have a more authentic dish, replace the tomatoes with chopped cucumbers.

Bulgur Wheat, Tomato and Mint Salad

1 cup bulgur wheat
2 cups warm water
2 cups fresh parsley, chopped
1 cup fresh mint, chopped
½ cup chopped onions
¼ cup olive oil
3 Tbs lemon juice
1 large tomato, diced
1 tsp salt, or to taste
1 tsp pepper, or to taste

Soak bulgur wheat in water until softened, usually 30-45 minutes. Drain any excess water and combine with parsley, mint, onions, olive oil, lemon juice, tomatoes and seasonings. Refrigerate. The longer you let the salad marinate, the better it will taste. I like to leave it overnight. Serve chilled with fresh pita bread. (See recipe for Simple Pita Bread on page 64.) Serves 4.

The Biblical Fruit Society of Israel

To meet today's market needs, most farmers in Israel grow fruit crops adapted from non-native varieties. The traditional varieties, those that have been cultivated in the region for thousands of years, are on the verge of extinction. The Biblical group is dedicated to identifying and preserving those species mentioned in the Bible and the Talmud. They do so by characterizing and comparing the DNA of those seeds to the seeds and other viable remains found in archeological sites. To learn more about their efforts, visit their Web page at: **agri.gov.il/Horticulture/Sataf/biblical-fruits.html**.

THE peach originated in China and spread through Asia to the Mediterranean. In eastern mythology, the peach has roughly the same role as the apple in western myth – as a symbol of immortality and knowledge. Peaches grew in the Middle East during biblical times.

Couscous with Peaches and Raisins

    1 tsp olive oil
    ½ cup chopped onions
    ½ cup grated carrot
    ⅓ cup diced tomato
    ¼ cup raisins
    ¼ cup golden raisins
    ½ cup chopped peaches
    2½ cups uncooked couscous
    1¾ cups chicken broth
    1 cup water
    1 tsp curry powder
    Salt and pepper to taste
    Mint for garnish

Sauté onions, carrot and tomato over medium heat

until soft, about 5 minutes. Add raisins, peaches and couscous. Stir for 1-2 minutes. Add broth, water, curry powder, salt and pepper. Bring to a boil. Cover and remove from heat. Let stand, without peeking, until all the liquid is absorbed. Toss and serve. Serves 4.

> *And Ahab spake unto Naboth, saying, Give me thy vineyard, that I may have it for a garden of herbs, because it is near unto my house: and I will give thee for it a better vineyard than it; or, if it seem good to thee, I will give thee the worth of it in money.*
> *— 1 Kings 21:2*

Tabbouleh with Grapes
- 1 cup bulgur wheat
- 2 cups warm water
- ¾ cup fresh cilantro, chopped fine
- 2 tsp garlic, minced
- 3 Tbs pistachios, chopped fine
- 1 Tbs grated lemon zest, chopped fine
- 2 Tbs olive oil
- 3 Tbs lemon juice
- 1½ cups seedless grapes

Place the bulgur wheat in a bowl and cover with water. Set aside until wheat is softened. Drain remaining water. Add all other ingredients and toss thoroughly. Refrigerate until ready to serve. The longer you let it marinate, the better it will be. Serves 4.

Legumes

And Jacob sod pottage: and Esau came from the field, and he was faint. And Esau said to Jacob, Feed me, I pray thee, with that same red pottage; for I am faint: Therefore was his name called Edom. And Jacob said, Sell me this day thy birthright. And Esau said, Behold, I am at the point to die: and what profit shall this birthright do to me? And Jacob said, Swear to me this day; and he sware unto him: and he sold his birthright unto Jacob. Then Jacob gave Esau bread and pottage of lentiles; and he did eat and drink, and rose up, and went his way: thus Esau despised his birthright.
– Genesis 25:29-34

Legumes are the pods of plants from the *Legumi-nosae* family that include peas, beans and vetch. The dry fruit releases its edible seeds by splitting along its seams. Legumes are consumed as food by humans and animals. They are very high in protein and soluble fiber, and when combined with vegetables and grains, they provide a balanced diet. They are easy to cultivate and can be made into a variety of soups and pottages. Boiled with garlic, they make an effective (if somewhat pungent) cough medicine.

They are easy to dry, and can be stored for a long time. During biblical times, the most popular legume was the lentil. Mentioned frequently in the story of David,

49

it is an ingredient in Ezekiel's Bread and Jacob's Pottage. In Egypt, Israel and other Middle Eastern countries, dried legumes are considered the best food to carry on a journey.

PEAS have been cultivated in the Middle East since about 7,000 B.C. One of the popular herbs to accompany them is mint. There are at least 30 species of mint, including the most common – peppermint and spearmint. All mint varieties have the property of preventing milk from curdling, and the ancients used it to help preserve milk a bit longer. In France, mint is still sometimes referred to as Menthe de Notre Dame (Mint of Our Lady) and in England, it is called Our Lady's Herb – both names which honor the Virgin Mary.

Mint Peas

> 1 lb fresh peas
> Water for boiling
> ¼ cup butter
> 2 Tbs mint, chopped
> 1 tsp sugar
> Salt and pepper to taste

Cook peas in boiling, lightly salted water until tender, about 5 minutes. Drain and set aside. In another saucepan, heat the butter until melted. Add the peas, mint and sugar. Toss gently and season to taste with salt and pepper. Serves 4.

Mint Peas and Couscous

> 1 cup water
> ¼ tsp salt
> Pepper to taste

¾ cup frozen peas
1 cup couscous
2 Tbs fresh mint, chopped
1 Tbs fresh lemon juice

Bring water to a boil. Add salt, pepper and peas and cook for 5 minutes. Add couscous, cover and remove from heat. Let stand, covered, until water is absorbed. Toss with mint and lemon juice. Chill and serve with additional lemon slices and seasonings so that your guests may adjust the taste. Serves 4.

CHICKPEAS (also known as garbanzo beans) are one of the most widespread and versatile legume. They can be eaten fresh, parched, fried, roasted or boiled. They're enjoyed as a snack food, a side dish and a sweet. Westerners encounter them frequently as hummus, a chickpea and sesame seed spread that is scooped up with wedges of pita bread. When I lived in Chicago, I would often get together with the neighbors for tea and conversation after work. When it was Lahab's turn to make the snack – he was from Iraq – he would provide homemade hummus and pita bread. Yum!

Hummus

1 15-oz can chickpeas
½ cup sesame seeds
2 cloves garlic
3 Tbs lemon juice
½ tsp salt
Parsley or mint for garnish
Pita bread

Drain chickpeas and reserve liquid. In a blender, combine liquid, sesame seeds and garlic. Add beans, lemon juice and salt. Beat on high until completely blended.

51

Pour onto a serving platter and garnish with parsley or mint. Dip pita bread directly into the communal dish.

Chickpeas with Greens

    1½ lbs fresh greens (spinach, dandelion, etc.)
    Olive oil
    1 Tbs minced garlic
    1 small onion, chopped fine
    ½ cup cooked chickpeas
    ½ tsp cumin
    ½ tsp coriander
    ¼ tsp saffron
    1 cup tomatoes, peeled and diced
    Salt and pepper to taste
    2 tsp lemon juice

Sauté the greens in a little olive oil. Drain greens and pat dry. Sauté garlic and onion in same oil (adding more if necessary) until tender. Add chickpeas and spices and heat through. Add greens and diced tomato. Cover and simmer until heated through, about 15 minutes. Add more oil if necessary to prevent from drying out. Just before serving, add lemon juice and toss. Serves 4 to 6.

FAVA beans are native to the Middle East, and archeological evidence indicates they were domesticated at least 9,000 years ago, making it one of the oldest cultivated crops! Use quickly spread through Asia, southern Europe and North Africa, where it is still popular today. The fava pod looks a bit like the green pea, but inside are six to eight beans that look like lima beans. The pods are edible when young, but most people wait until the beans mature. The U.S. has many fava bean fields, primarily in New Jersey and California.

This dish is sometimes called Egyptian chili (at least that's how it appeared on the menus in Cairo) and is said to have been a favorite of King Ramses III.

Spiced Fava Beans

1 16-oz can fava beans
1 large yellow onion, diced
1 tomato, diced
1½ Tbs olive oil
1 tsp cumin
¼ cup parsley, chopped
4 Tbs lemon juice
Pinch of chili pepper
Salt and pepper to taste

Add beans to pot and heat according to package directions. Add all remaining ingredients and simmer another 5 or 10 minutes, adjusting seasoning to taste. Served with pita bread. Serves 2.

Note: A more authentic version can be made by leaving out the tomato. Many cooks also skip using onion and opt for a bit of minced garlic instead.

ESAU must have surely been faint with hunger to sell his birthright for a bowl of soup and bread. Or maybe this soup is simply that good! Unfortunately, the exact ingredients of Jacob's pottage are lost to the ages, but there are several Middle Eastern versions of red lentil soup that may be descended from the original. Esau is nicknamed Edom which means red. It's also the  name for the lands south of Moab and was probably derived from the fields of red lentils that once grew there.

Jacob's Pottage

⅔ cup red lentils (available at Middle Eastern
grocery stores)

1 medium yellow onion, peeled and diced

1 Tbs flour

¼ cup wild rice

2 Tbs olive oil

2 tsp salt

¼ tsp black pepper

¼ cup diced bell pepper

5 cups water

2 Tbs lemon juice

2 Tbs parsley, chopped

Pinch of red pepper

Place lentils, onion, flour, rice, olive oil, salt, pepper and bell pepper in a large soup pot. Toss well and carefully add the water. Bring to a boil. Reduce heat and let simmer, covered, for an hour. Pour soup into a blender and beat until creamy and smooth. Stir in lemon juice, parsley and red pepper. Serve hot. Serves 2.

Note: Instead of water, some cooks use chicken, beef or lamb broth and omit the lemon juice. If you want a vegetarian dish, stick with the water. Other people add fruit such as apricots, which also makes for a tasty dish. There's plenty of room to experiment — just imagine what Jacob might have had on hand to make Esau's mouth water!

I DIDN'T discover spinach until I was 18 years old and living on my own. The only way I had ever eaten it was from those frozen packages. It wasn't until I was doing my own grocery shopping that I learned the best way to eat fresh spinach — raw or in soups.

Spinach and Lentil Soup

1½ cups lentils
7 cups water
1 medium sweet onion, peeled and chopped
1 small zucchini, peeled and diced
2 tsp minced garlic
¼ cup olive oil
1 cup fresh, chopped spinach
1 tsp salt, or to taste
Pepper to taste
¼ cup lemon juice

Bring lentils and water to a boil. Reduce heat, cover and simmer until tender. Sauté onions, zucchini and garlic in olive oil. Add spinach and season to taste with salt and pepper. Add sautéed onions and return to a boil. Add lemon juice and simmer for 10 minutes. Serves 4.

Bread and Whole Grain

The cultivation of grain is said to be the true beginning of civilization. Grain was first planted, harvested, ground into flour and baked into bread in the region of the Fertile Crescent, where lie the modern countries of Israel, Jordan, Iran, Iraq, Turkey and Lebanon.

The first bread was probably made 12,000 or so years ago by combining coarsely crushed grain and water. This "dough" was then heated on hot stones and baked by covering it with a layer of ashes.

The job of baker is one of the oldest trades in the world. Loaves of bread, perfectly preserved, that were found in Egyptian tombs can be seen at the British Museum in London. These 5,000-year-old loaves and rolls are an eerie link to our distant ancestors.

It was the Egyptians who accidentally discovered that when they allowed wheat dough to ferment with wild yeast that was in the air, a gas that made a light, expandable loaf formed. Wheat quickly became the grain of choice over others grown in the region, although barley was grown by necessity because it was easier to cultivate in the poor soil and dry climate.

Herodotus (484-424 B.C.) describes millet that grew in the hanging gardens of Babylon, and Isaiah mentions that rye was sown at the border of barley and wheat fields. These grains were very nutritious. Einkorn wheat, which still grows wild in the Middle East, has 1.5 times as much protein as modern wheat varieties. There is some speculation that the Egyptians also developed the first ovens.

All evidence indicates that during Bible times breadmaking was women's work, a task usually performed early in the morning. Grinding was done by hand using a mull (a type of bowl) and a millstone. Most families had their own. The bread was leavened – caused to rise – with a leavening agent similar to a sourdough starter. It could be baked directly in the ashes of the fire as shown in John 21:9, "As soon as they were come to land, they saw a fire of coals there, and fish laid thereon, and bread." The bread could also be placed on hot stones, which was more sanitary considering that kindling often consisted of animal droppings.

Bakeries existed where rich and poor alike could purchase loaves or bring their own loaves to be cooked in communal ovens. The quick exodus of the Israelites from Egypt prevented them from baking bread in the usual manner – they were unable to let it rise. Today, Jews commemorate the Exodus by eating unleavened bread.

Although it is said that "man shall not live by bread alone," bread was long thought to be the one food essential for survival, and the acts of baking and eating bread often took on a magical significance. This "bread magic" could appear in many forms, from speaking charms over bread about to be eaten to baking it into all sorts of shapes and effigies. Early Christians would mark their loaves with crosses – a modern equivalent is the Hot Cross Buns served on Good Friday.

> *At that time Jesus went on the Sabbath day through the corn; and his disciples were an hungered, and began to pluck the ears of corn, and to eat. – Matthew 12:1*

Bible Porridge

In the days of Jesus, the cultivation of grains such as wheat and barley was already well-established. Travelers could take handfuls of grain from the fields they passed as long as they didn't use any tools – helping yourself was not a crime!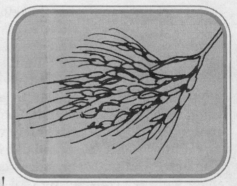
(Just try that nowadays. When I was a kid I used to get chased out of my neighbor's strawberry patch with a pepper gun!)

Although people of the biblical era sometimes ate grain right from the stalk, it was not ideal. Raw grain is difficult to digest.

After harvesting and threshing, the kernels would be stored until needed. It was not ground in advance, but only when it was needed because whole grain keeps better than milled grain. Whole kernels also hold on to their nutritional value longer, so bread baked from freshly ground grain was healthier than bread baked from stored flour.

Baking grain into bread isn't the only way to eat it. It could be parched, roasted, boiled in soups or tossed in salads. Grain could also be soaked in milk or water and then boiled, sweetened and spiced to form a type of porridge. References to such recipes stretch to the dawn of time.

THE following porridge recipes are simple enough to have been used by biblical era cooks!

Roasted Porridge

Roasted Porridge is made from hulled barley grains. Place grains in a pot by the fire and let them roast. Hand grind grains in a *quern* (a type of hand mill). Place the meal in a bowl, heat some milk, and pour over. Serve hot.

Oat Wine Porridge

Place a cup of uncooked oats in a broad, deep pan and cover with water. Stir and let stand for 12 hours. Pour off the liquid. Cover with fresh water and let stand for another 12 hours. Repeat one more time. Remove water. Pour oatmeal into a saucepan. Heat and stir continuously until it bubbles and thickens, adding more water if necessary. Pour into dishes. When cool, turn out onto plates and serve with milk or wine and sugar.

Cracked Porridge

Fill a jar halfway with wheat grains, cover with milk and set in a warm spot for 12 hours. The grains that swell and burst are known as creed wheat. Use the creed wheat to make a Cracked Wheat Porridge that can be served with cream and honey.

ESSENE bread gets its name from the Essenes, an ancient Jewish sect whose members may have included both John the Baptist and Jesus. Many Essenes were said to be healers, and folklore said they could cast out demons, cure illnesses and raise the dead. Many of their values – poverty, austerity, meditation – were adopted by the early church.

Originally, this bread would have been baked on hot rocks under the blazing Middle Eastern sun. A slow oven and a lot of patience (this bread takes several days to make) will get you a decent result. My friend Angela calls this basic wheat sprout bread "Bible Bread," and the name has stuck.

Essene Bread

3 cups hard wheat berries
Water to cover
Sesame seeds

Soak hard wheat in a jar, covered with water, overnight. The kernels will soak up a significant amount of water. Transfer to a colander, rinse and set aside to sprout. This will take about two days. Rinse periodically with cold water to keep from drying out. When ready, the shoot should be approximately the same length as the berry, perhaps a bit longer. Grind in a food processor or meat grinder, not a blender. Turn onto a clean surface and knead for about five or ten minutes. Form two loaves. Sprinkle sesame seeds on a cookie sheet and place your loaves on top of them. Sprinkle seeds on the surface of the loaves as well, if desired. Bake at 250°F for approximately 3½ hours. Your sprout bread is finished when the bottom is no longer soft.

Because of its high moisture content, store this in the refrigerator if you do not eat it right away.

Take thou also unto thee wheat, and barley,
and beans, and lentiles, and millet, and

*fitches, and put them in one vessel, and
make thee bread thereof, according to the
number of the days that thou shalt lie upon
thy side, three hundred and ninety days
shall thou eat thereof.*
– Ezekiel 4:9

THIS recipe for bread was told to Ezekiel by God. Unfortunately, Ezekiel does not provide us with exact measurements, so what follows is a modern reconstruction given to me by a friend in Scotland. I've adjusted the measurements for an American audience, but please feel free to experiment with the ingredients yourself. Leave your heart and mind open for guidance as you prepare this bread – many people say they feel closer to God in the simple act of baking.

Ezekiel Bread

- 4 cups lukewarm water
- ½ cup olive oil
- 1 cup honey
- 2 packages active dry yeast
- 3 cups whole wheat berries
- 1 cup rye flour
- ½ cup barley
- ½ cup millet
- ¼ cup dry green lentils
- ½ cup assorted, dried beans (soy, kidney, pinto, navy, etc.
- 2 Tbs salt, or to taste
- Fitches*

Combine water, olive oil, honey and yeast in a large mixing bowl. Be sure that the water is not too hot, or it will kill the yeast. (Baby formula temperature is just about right.) Set aside for 10 minutes. Combine all remaining ingredients in a flour mill. Add to the yeast mixture and blend well. It should have the consistency of a batter bread. Divide dough into two greased and floured 9x5-inch bread loaf pans. Cover and let rise for 1 hour or until doubled in size. (Do not punch down.) Bake at 350°F for 50 minutes. Loaves are done when they are a rich, golden brown.

There is much debate over what is meant by "fitches." It was probably meant to be an herb, and nutmeg, fennel, and cumin have been recommended by various cooks. Use whichever one inspires you. I used fennel because I had some left in my kitchen, and the breads were quite tasty.

MANY people think that white bread, which has a refined texture and smooth taste, is a modern development over coarser, whole-grain "peasant" breads. However, white bread has been around in one form or another for at least 2,000 years. The Romans, whose empire covered much of the known world during the biblical era, had a preference for white bread, as noted by Pliny (A.D. 70), "The wheat of Cyprus is swarthy, and makes a bread that is dark. For this reason it is often mixed with the white wheat of Alexandria."

Roman Bread

- 1 packet dry yeast
- 1 cup lukewarm water, plus ⅓ cup
- 3 to 3½ cups flour
- 2 tsp salt
- 1 Tbs butter, melted
- 1 Tbs sesame seeds

Sprinkle yeast in ⅓ cup water. Stir lightly and set aside for several minutes. Sift together half the flour and the salt, then add the yeast mixture. Work together, adding more flour until you have a dough that is workable, but still slightly sticky. Place dough in a greased bowl, turning once to coat all sides. Let it rest for 15 minutes. Knead the dough on a lightly floured surface for 15 minutes until smooth and elastic. Add a little more flour if necessary so that the dough is no longer sticky. Return the dough to your greased bowl, cover, set in a warm spot and let it triple in size. Be patient – this will take several hours. Punch the dough down and divide into four balls. Grease a glass baking pan and sprinkle sesame seeds on the surface of the pan before placing each of the dough balls in the pan. Flatten slightly to form a classic round bread shape and mark with a cross if desired. Brush with melted butter and bake at 400°F for 30 minutes. Bread is done when it is a lovely golden color, and a "tap test" sounds hollow. Serve hot with spiced butter.

And when ye reap the harvest of your land,
thou shalt not make clean riddance of the

corners of thy field when thou reapest, nei-
ther shalt thou gather any gleaning of thy
harvest: thou shalt leave them unto the poor,
and to the stranger: I am the Lord your God.
— Leviticus 23:22

ACCORDING to the civil code found in Leviticus, the corners of a farmer's field were not to be harvested. Any grain that was left behind was to remain in the field for passing travelers or the poor. When I was living in Minnesota, I saw many farmers who would let the poor come in to glean strawberries from the fields or apples from the orchard after the official harvest was past. A great number of families, who otherwise might not have been able to, could provide fresh fruit for their families and share in the harvest.

THIS recipe for pita bread is very basic and easy to make. It's great to have on hand for unexpected guests.

Simple Pita Bread

2 tsp dry yeast
1 cup lukewarm water
½ tsp salt, or to taste
3 cups all-purpose flour

Dissolve the yeast in warm water. Be sure that the water is not too hot, or it will kill the yeast. (Baby formula temperature is just about right.) Combine yeast, water, salt and flour into a dough. Knead for approximately five minutes. Cover and let rise in a warm spot until tripled in size. Divide dough into six portions and shape each into a ball. Pat each round into a circle that is about ½-inch thick. Bake at 350°F for 10 minutes until golden brown. Great for dipping into sauces or with hummus.

House of Bread

In Hebrew, Bethlehem means "House of Bread." It was home to Ruth and the birthplace of both David and Jesus.

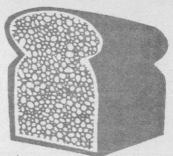

Jesus was considered the bread of life, "Then Jesus said unto them, Verily, verily, I say unto to you, Moses gave you not that bread from heaven; but my Father giveth you the true bread from heaven. For the bread of God is he which cometh down from heaven, and giveth life unto the world. Then said they unto him, Lord, evermore give us this bread. And Jesus said unto them, I am the bread of life: he that cometh to me shall never hunger; and he that believeth on me shall never thirst." (John 6:32-35)

Whole-Wheat Pita Bread

- 2 tsp active dry yeast
- 2½ cups warm water
- 3 cups whole wheat flour
- 3 cups all-purpose flour
- 2 tsp salt
- 1 Tbs olive oil

Sprinkle yeast into water. Be sure that the water is not too hot, or it will kill the yeast. (Baby formula temperature is just about right.) Set aside for five minutes and then stir in half of the flour, one cup at a time, until blended. Set aside for 30 minutes. Add salt and blend in the olive oil. Add remaining flour, a cup at a time. Turn dough onto floured surface and knead until smooth and elastic, about 10 to 15 minutes. Place dough in a lightly greased bowl, turning once to coat all sides. Cover and let rise until double. Preheat oven to 450°F, placing unglazed quarry tiles (or small baking sheets) on the bottom rack of your oven. Punch down dough and divide into 16 equal balls. Flatten each piece to form rounds that are ¼-inch thick. Place breads on oven tiles and bake for 5 minutes or so, until the breads balloon. Remove from the oven and set aside while you bake the remaining breads. *Pitot* (the plural for pita) will puff up while cooking and flatten while cooling. You can cut them in half and fill with any number of goodies or tear and dip them in your favorite sauce.

THE Roman army enjoyed all kinds of bread, and each one seemed to be baked with a special purpose in mind. "Oyster bread" was to be eaten with oysters, and other special breads were made with spices.

Hardtack, or flatbread, has been eaten for thousands of years. Traditional hardtack is made from little more than a 2:1 proportion of flour and water, with a pinch of salt thrown in for flavor. Its nickname, "Teeth Dullers," is an adequate description. It often needed to be softened in a liquid before being edible – thrown on top of soups or dunked in hot ale or pork fat. But it was easy to pack and transport and would last a long time, making it a favorite of armies on the move.

Flatbread

> 4 cups rye flour
> Hearty pinch of salt to taste
> 1½ cups water

Combine flour and salt. Bring water to a boil and carefully moisten flour/salt mixture. Knead until blended and roll into thin, round cakes about 7 or 8 inches across. Bake on a cast-iron griddle, turning frequently. Break into serving pieces about the size of crackers and

66

serve with butter, cheese, hummus, smoked fish or smoked meats.

And when Gideon was come, behold, there was a man that told a dream unto his fellow, and said, Behold I dreamed a dream, and, lo, a cake of barley bread tumbled into the host of Midian and came unto a tent, and smote it that it fell, and overturned it, that the tent lay along.
– Judges 7:13

ROUND loaves of bread have been popular in Middle Eastern and Mediterranean cultures for centuries. The shape came from the ceramic bowls that the dough was set to rise in.

Barley Bread

- 1 pkg dry yeast
- 3 tsp brown sugar
- 1 cup warm water
- 2 cups barley flour, divided
- 1 Tbs olive oil
- 1 tsp salt, or to taste
- ⅓ cup fava bean flour

Combine yeast with ½ tsp of the brown sugar and water in a large mixing bowl. Set aside for five minutes. Stir in 1 cup of the barley flour along with remaining sugar, olive oil and salt. Add fava bean flour and the rest of barley flour. Turn dough onto a lightly floured surface and knead for about 10 minutes, until you have a dough that is smooth and elastic. Divide dough in half and form two round loaves. Mark a cross on each one by pressing a knife into the surface. Let rise until doubled and bake at 350°F for one hour. Makes two loaves.

Good Friday Bread

Some people will still admit to the belief that the buns baked on Good Friday will never get moldy and can be used in various charms to combat illness. It used to be the custom that at least one was kept from each year's baking for medicinal use. It was hung in the kitchen and allowed to dry out thoroughly, then powdered and mixed in a glass of milk, water or ale to be given to the ill person.

Unleavened Bread

1 cup whole wheat flour
¼ tsp salt
1 Tbs butter
2 Tbs oil
¼ cup water

Sift together flour, salt and butter. The mixture will be crumbly. Combine oil and water and blend into the flour mixture. Combine thoroughly. Knead on a lightly floured surface. Roll out as thin as possible. Prick in several spots and bake at 400°F for 8 to 10 minutes.

Vinegar Bread

- 3 cups flour
- ¼ tsp baking powder
- 1 cup water
- 1 cup clarified butter, melted (see page 35)
- ¼ tsp salt, or to taste
- 2 tsp sugar
- 1 tsp white vinegar

Combine flour and baking powder. Beat in water, 1 Tbs of the butter, salt, sugar and vinegar. On a lightly floured surface, knead for 10 minutes to form a dough that is smooth and elastic. Divide dough into 6 round balls and allow to rest, covered, for 15 minutes. With lightly floured hands, pat each ball into a 6-inch round. Brush with melted butter and roll up like a cinnamon roll. Let bread rest for another 15 minutes before flattening it out again. (Rolling increases the flakiness of this bread.) Brush the surface with melted butter and roll it up again. Repeat this process a total of 4 times, waiting approximately 15 minutes in between each cycle. Pat each bread into a circle and fry on both sides until you have a bread that is rich and golden. This bread is traditionally dipped in honey.

Doth the plowman plow all day to sow?
Doth he open and break the clods of his
ground? When he hath made plain the
face thereof, doth he not cast abroad
the fitches, and scatter the cummin,
and cast in the principal wheat
and the appointed barley and
the rye in their place?
— Isaiah 28:24-25

Meat and Poultry

These are the beasts which ye shall eat among all the beasts that are on the earth. Whatsoever parteth the hoof, and is cloven-footed, and cheweth the cud, among the beasts, that shall ye eat.
— Leviticus 11:2-3

Ancient people were vegetarians by necessity. When they did consume meat, it was usually a small animal – a goat, sheep or "fatted calf" – and only for special occasions. Cows, bulls or camels were reserved for large holiday feasts when there would be little chance of leftovers. After all, there were few ways to preserve and store meat.

The ancients did eat poultry, including ducks, hens and geese. Levitical code prevented them from eating birds of prey or carrion eaters, although other wild birds could be eaten. To this day, quail, partridge and pigeon are popular Middle Eastern delicacies. Cairo is the only modern city I've been to where I never saw a single pigeon in the streets. My friend Stephanie and I would joke that it was because they were all destined for the roaster!

Venison Stew

2 Tbs lard
2 lbs venison, cubed
Salt and pepper to taste
Water
Miscellaneous vegetables

Melt lard in soup pot. Season venison with salt and pepper and add to the pot. Sear meat. Cover with water and bring to a boil. Reduce heat and let simmer 45 minutes. Add vegetables of your choice and simmer for another 45 minutes, until all vegetables are tender. Serve hot with fresh bread to sop up the juices. Serves 4.

SHEEP are the first animal mentioned in the Bible by name. They were a very important possession, valued for their high-fat content. They were often used for sacrifice, although they later came to be a symbol for Jesus, for the church and for God's chosen people.

Leg of lamb is a common dish and can be simply prepared by seasoning with salt and pepper. Or you can add a host of spices as seen below.

Leg of Lamb

    1 large leg of lamb
    12 cardamom seeds
    4 sticks cinnamon, broken in smaller pieces
    4 cloves garlic
    1 tsp saffron
    Juice of 1 lemon
    2 dried lemons (available at health food stores
        or Middle Eastern groceries, also called
        preserved lemons)
    ½ tsp allspice
    2 tsp salt, or to taste
    ¼ tsp pepper, or to taste
    1 cup plain yogurt
    6½ cups water, hot
    ¼ cup vegetable oil
    ½ cup slivered, blanched almonds
    ⅔ cup currants

Make several small slices in the leg of lamb and stuff

with cardamom seeds, cinnamon and 2 of the garlic cloves which have been sliced for this purpose. Soak the saffron in lemon juice. Meanwhile, grind the dried lemon with the other two garlic cloves, allspice, salt and pepper. Blend together saffron mixture and dried lemon mixture with yogurt. Spread the yogurt mixture on the leg of lamb and let rest in a cool spot for 20 minutes. As the meat rests, prepare your baking pan by pouring in the hot water and the oil. Place meat in roasting pan. Cover with tin foil and bake at 350°F for 2½ hours. Uncover and let meat brown. When serving, sprinkle with almonds and currants as a garnish. Great with steamed vegetables. Serves 4-6.

SHISH kabobs are very versatile – you can adapt the recipe to meet your needs. Don't like eggplant? Don't use it. Replace it with a vegetable you like. The name Shish Kabob is Turkish and means "skewered meat." People throughout the Middle East enjoy this meat-on-a-stick dish which is quick to prepare and can be cooked directly over an open fire.

Shish Kabob

> 2 lbs leg of lamb, cubed
> 1 large sweet onion, peeled and sliced
> 3 plum tomatoes, sliced
> 1 Tbs olive oil
> Juice of one lemon or lime
> Salt and pepper to taste

1 green pepper, sliced
1 eggplant

Toss meat, onion and tomato with olive oil and lemon or lime juice. Season with salt and pepper and marinate in the refrigerator overnight. Arrange meat on skewers, add green pepper and eggplant slices. Broil over grill or in oven until meat is cooked through. Serves 4.

Beef and Date Stew

2 lbs beef, cubed
1 stick butter
1 large sweet onion, peeled and chopped
1 Tbs minced garlic
½ tsp cinnamon
Salt and pepper to taste
Water
1½ cups dates, pitted and chopped
1 cup wild rice

Sauté the beef in the butter until it begins to brown. Add the onions and garlic and continue to simmer until vegetables soften. Add cinnamon, salt and pepper. Cover with water and cook over medium flame for about 45 minutes. Add more water if any of the ingredients poke above the surface. Stir in the dates and rice and continue to cook over medium heat until the rice is cooked through. Serves 4-6.

Fish

As soon then as they were come to land, they saw a fire of coals there, and fish laid thereon, and bread. Jesus saith unto them, Bring of the fish which ye have now caught. Simon Peter went up, and drew the net to land full of great fishes, an hundred and fifty and three: and for all there were so many, yet was not the net broken.
— John 21:9-11

Although Jesus' first disciples were fishermen, the Hebrews were not a seafaring people. Fishing on the Sea of Galilee and the River Jordan was a big business, so those who lived nearby could eat fresh fish. Jerusalem received its fish supply from the Mediterranean, and the people who lived there enjoyed both fresh- and salt-

water species. Some of that fish would be sun-dried, pickled or salted, the only ways that fish could be preserved for any length of time.

The fish became an early symbol for Christ because the Greek word for fish, *ichthys*, was seen as an acronym for "Jesus Christ, Son of God." A medieval hymn calls Christ, "the little fish which the Virgin caught."

The Christian church established the custom of meatless Fridays, when fish would be the main course as part of a holy fast. Friday was also the sacred day of the pagan goddess Venus, and fish were eaten on Fridays in her honor. Perhaps that is why fish are still considered an aphrodisiac in many Western cultures.

Fish with Garlic and Tahini

**4 medium-sized whitefish, cleaned and
  split lengthwise
Salt and pepper to taste
Olive oil
1 large onion, peeled and chopped
3 cups tahini
¼ cup warm water
¾ cup fresh lemon juice
1 Tbs minced garlic
Pine nuts or almonds for garnish
Dash of cayenne pepper**

Season fish inside and out and brush with olive oil. Bake at 350°F for 20 minutes. Meanwhile, sauté onions in oil until golden. Add to fish. Combine tahini with water, lemon juice and garlic. Pour over fish and continue to bake for another 20 minutes. Garnish with pine nuts or almonds and a dash of cayenne pepper. Great with fresh bread. Serves 4.

Charbroiled Fish

**4 medium-sized whitefish, cleaned and
split lengthwise**
¼ to ½ cup butter, melted
Salt and pepper to taste

Brush fish with butter and season with salt and pepper. The fish can be placed directly on the grid of a grill or encased in a long-handled wire fish cooker. Either method will require the grid to be well-buttered. Broil the fish approximately 4 minutes per side. Baste generously with butter while grilling. Serves 4.

IN JEWISH folklore, the fish has been a symbol of fertility ever since Jacob gave his children a blessing that they should multiply like fish in the sea. Fish are also associated with the coming of the Messiah. According to a legend, the Messiah will come in the form of a great fish from the sea.

Red Snapper

**6 red snapper
fillets**
**Salt and pepper
to taste**
1 large sweet onion
½ Tbs minced garlic
1 Tbs olive oil
**1 large red pepper, grilled,
skinned and chopped**
Dash of cayenne pepper
1 small bunch mint leaves
½ Tbs dried thyme
3 Tbs fresh lemon juice

Rub fish with salt and pepper and place in baking pan. Sauté onion and garlic in olive oil until softened. Add remaining ingredients; blend thoroughly. Pour over fish and bake at 350°F for 20 minutes. Excellent when served with bread or couscous. Serves 6.

So they took up Jonah, and cast him forth into the sea: and the sea ceased from her raging. Then the men feared the Lord exceedingly, and offered a sacrifice unto the Lord, and made vows. Now the Lord had prepared a great fish to swallow up Jonah. And Jonah was in the belly of the fish three days and three nights.
– Jonah 1:15-17

Jonah and the Great Fish

Can a man be swallowed by a fish and survive? There are several documented cases of people who have been swallowed by giant fish or whales and who have survived the encounter to tell about it.

There is one species of fish that lives in the Mediterranean, *Carharodon carcharias* (Sea Dog), that can grow to a length of 50 feet! Sperm whales are able to swallow entire squids and sharks, and shark skeletons of 16 feet (nearly three times the height of a human!) have been found in their stomachs.

One widely circulated story claims that in 1891 a sailor named James Bartley fell overboard from the whaling ship *Star of the East* somewhere near the Falkland Islands. Forty-eight hours later, a whale was harpooned and dragged aboard ship, and Bartley was found within. Supposedly his skin was bleached pale by the gastric juices, but otherwise he suffered no lasting damage. While most scholars claim this particular story is nothing but an urban legend, there are other stories that may support the theory.

As reported in *The Princeton Theological Review*, in 1758 a sailor fell overboard and was swallowed whole by just such a fish. A cannon was fired at the fish, and when struck, it vomited the man up, scared and shaking but none the worse for wear.

The choice to believe such encounters is yours, but one thing's for sure – Jonah probably never ate another fish for as long as he lived.

Insects

We may cringe at the thought, but eating bugs is not uncommon in other parts of the world. In fact, the eating of bugs has an official name – *entomophagy*. The most commonly consumed bug the world over is the grasshopper (also called the locust), and it's one of the few allowed by the Bible. The New Testament says John the Baptist "did eat locusts and wild honey." (Mark 1:6)

Nowadays in the United States, they are only sold in gourmet food shops, but hoppers were once eaten by Native American tribes and early European settlers. They were often dried and served whole or ground into flour and used in a variety of recipes. I inadvertently sampled them at the University of Iowa.

I was served a batch of chocolate-chip cookies I thought contained nuts – but I was wrong! Those crunchy bits were, in fact, oven-dried grasshoppers. Don't knock 'em 'til you try 'em.

Grasshoppers are high in protein – nearly 15 grams per insect – and very low in fat.

THIS is considered the most humane way of preparing grasshoppers:

Dry-Roasted Grasshoppers

Start with 24 live insects. Place them in a colander and cover with cheesecloth. Rinse with lukewarm water and place in the freezer. After 20 minutes or so, they will be dead but not frozen. Remove the head, wings and hind legs. Spread them on a cookie sheet and bake at 200°F for 2 hours, until they are dried. You can use them in the recipes below or dip them directly into melted chocolate or warmed honey.

Dry-Roasted Grasshopper Flour

Follow the method for preparing dry-roasted grasshoppers. Grind them in a flour mill.

HERE'S a modern recipe equivalent for John the Baptist's honey-covered locusts.

Grasshopper Carmel Corn

> 10 cups popped corn
> 1 cup dry-roasted grasshoppers, crushed
> ½ cup butter
> ¼ cup corn syrup
> 1 cup packed brown sugar
> ½ tsp salt
> ½ tsp baking soda

Pop corn and pour into an oven-proof container. Add grasshoppers. Combine butter, corn syrup, sugar and salt in a medium saucepan. Heat over medium flame until bubbly around the edges, stirring occasionally. Continue to cook for 5 minutes over medium heat. Remove from flame and add baking soda. Stir until foamy – mixture will double in size. Pour over popped corn and grasshoppers. Mix well. Bake at 200°F for 1 hour, stirring every 10 minutes. Serves 4 – although it may be hard to find even one volunteer!

Fruited Grasshoppers

> 1 cup grasshopper flour (previous page)
> 1 Tbs raisins
> ½ cup dried mixed fruit (apricots, dates, etc.), chopped
> ¼ cup water

Combine all ingredients. Pinch off pieces of dough to make strips about the size of your finger and place on greased baking sheets. Bake for 20 minutes at 325°F. An excellent energy bar. Makes about 12 pieces.

Honey

*And their father Israel
said unto them, If it
must be so now, do
this; take of the best
fruits in the land in
your vessels, and carry
down the man a present, a
little balm, and a little honey, spices, and
myrrh, nuts and almonds.*
— Genesis 43:11

Centuries before sugar became widely available, sweet honey was used to enhance the flavor and palatability of foods. Prehistoric paintings depict early man gathering wild honey in much the same manner as it is gathered today.

Honey was one of the few preservatives known to the ancients. In addition to its use as a food additive, it was also considered a powerful source of resurrection magic. Pagan tribes in the Mediterranean once placed their dead in a fetal position and embalmed them in a jar of honey so that they could await a rebirth in heaven. Christian mythology says that bees have their origin in the tears Christ shed during the crucifixion.

In the Bible, "honey" can refer to the product of bees or to a sweet syrup made from grapes or dates.

The Great Medicine

Honey is not just good, it's good for you. An ancient Egyptian scroll listed more than 500 remedies that include honey as one of the ingredients. Modern science backs up this folk wisdom. Honey has been proven to kill harmful bacteria in the digestive tract and when rubbed into minor wounds, it helps them heal faster. A tablespoon of honey in a glass of milk at bedtime can help fight insomnia, and there is promising new research that it can help alleviate asthma symptoms.

> *Pleasant words are as an honeycomb, sweet to the soul, and health to the bones.*
> *— Proverbs 16:24*

MANY different herbs can be used to flavor honey. Among the most interesting are lavender, thyme, rosemary, mint, bay, linden, cinnamon, basil, lemon verbena, rose geranium and lemon geranium.

Herbed Honey

1 cup honey
1 sprig or several leaves of the fresh herb of your choice

Heat the honey gently over low heat. Place the herbs in a clean jar and pour the warm honey over them. Seal and allow to mellow for at least a week before using.

Honey Butter

½ cup butter
¼ cup honey
½ tsp lemon zest

Soften butter to room temperature. Stir in honey and lemon zest. Serve with bread or meat.

> *Judah, and the land of Israel, they were thy merchants: they traded in thy market wheat of Minnith and Pannag, and honey, and oil, and balm.*
> *— Ezekiel 27:17*

Honey Wine

½ cup honey
1 bottle dry white wine

Combine honey and wine. It is easier to blend in the honey if it has been heated first. Chill and serve.

Honey Yogurt

1 pint plain or vanilla yogurt
½ cup wildflower honey

Combine ingredients and serve.

SWEET and delicious cakes are as popular in Israel now as they were 9,000 years ago, when the citizens of Jericho dipped unleavened bread in spiced honey. There are more than 1,500 references to honey cakes in the Old and New Testament as well as the Islamic holy book, the Koran.

Biblical scholars credit this long love of sweet cakes for two reasons – bees, and thus honey, have always been plentiful in the region and the art of baking has been around for many, many thousands of years.

In Old Testament times, street vendors sold cakes similar to the modern baklava enjoyed throughout the Middle East and Mediterranean countries.

Baklava

Butter for coating the pan
1 cup ground almonds
1 cup ground walnuts
½ cup ground pistachios
2 tsp cinnamon
8 sheets phylo pastry
¼ cup butter, melted
1½ cups date sugar (see page 87)
2 Tbs grated lemon zest
3 Tbs lemon juice
2-3 Tbs maple syrup

Combine almonds, walnuts, pistachios and cinnamon. Cut each sheet of phylo in half and stack like paper. Brush melted butter on the first sheet and place in greased baking pan. Evenly sprinkle with some of the nut mixture. Repeat with remaining phylo sheets, creating thin layers and ending with a sheet of pastry. Cut in diagonal wedges and bake at 300°F for 30-40 minutes. Meanwhile, simmer date sugar, lemon zest, lemon juice and maple syrup until thickened. Pour on baklava and serve. Makes 24 pieces.

My son, eat thou honey, because it is good;
and the honeycomb, which is sweet
to thy taste.
– Proverbs 24:13

Dates and Figs

*For lo, the winter is past, the rain is over
and gone; the flowers appear on the earth;
the time of the singing of birds is come,
and the voice of the turtle is heard in our
land. The fig tree putteth forth her green
figs, and the vines with the tender
grape give a good smell. Arise, my love, my
fair one, and come away.*
— Song of Solomon 2:11-13

To the ancients, date palm trees provided more than just a nutritious and delicious staple fruit. Every part of the tree was used. The leaves were used as roofing tiles and woven into mats, baskets or any number of other useful household items. The fibers could be carved into needles. Date enthusiasts say there were over 365 different uses for the tree – you could go through an entire year and never create the same thing twice.

The city of Jericho was surrounded by fields of date palms that were well-established in the biblical era. A date palm tree is said to have given shelter to the Virgin Mary when she gave birth to Jesus and the sweet dates were said to have helped ease her labor pains.

Muslims consider the date palm to be the tree of life, for it was created from the dust left over from the creation of man. The prophet Muhammad often fasted on a diet of water and dates.

The date tree grew abundantly in ancient Israel until around the 13th century. After that, the date trees in that region became extinct. It was not until the midtwentieth century that date palm production started again. One man, Ben-Zion Yisraeli, is said to have traveled throughout the Middle East to collect sapling date trees and bring them back to the biblical homeland.

Dates are becoming more popular in this country and can be found at most grocery stores when in season. Look for the large, plump Medjool variety.

Date Sugar

Date sugar, made from dehydrated date pieces, is available at most Middle Eastern and Indian grocery stores as well as some specialty food stores. You may also try searching the Internet for "dry natural sweeteners" or "date sugar" to find other sources.

It is more nutritious than sugar and an excellent source of fiber. It can be substituted for brown or white sugar. Try it in breads, pies and cookies.

BIBLICAL scholars say the poet in Song of Solomon is referring to walnuts when he mentions a "garden of nuts." In this delicious dish, dates are paired with walnuts. It's hard to know where the walnut tree came from, but the ancient Romans thought it came from Persia. It was well-known throughout the Roman empire, and its Latin name is *Juglans regia*, the royal nut of Jupiter. Indeed, it was thought to be the food of the gods.

Walnut Dates

- 1 cup sesame seeds
- 1 lb fresh dates
- 1 can shelled walnuts
- 1 cup powdered sugar
- 1 cup cinnamon
- Nutmeg for sprinkling

Preheat oven 275°F. Dry roast the sesame seeds in oven or in a cast-iron frying pan. Carefully slice open one side of each date, being careful not to slice too far or the date will split completely in half. Remove the pit and fill the cavity with walnuts. Place dates in a round baking dish. Between each layer, sprinkle powdered sugar, cinnamon and sesame seeds. Sprinkle nutmeg on top. Place in oven and heat through – it will take only a few minutes. Can also be eaten cold. Serves 4 to 6.

Dates in Sweet Syrup

2 lbs fresh dates, Medjool or similar variety
2 cups water
2 cups sugar
Blanched almonds
Whole cloves

Peel the dates and cover them with boiling water. Cook until tender. Drain in a sieve and set aside to dry – do not discard cooking water. Push out pits with a knitting needle, ice pick or similar instrument. Layer dates in heavy pan, sprinkling sugar between each layer. Let stand, covered, overnight. Remove dates, leaving as much sugar as possible in the pan. Add the date-soaking water to the sugar, whisking briskly, and bring to a boil. Continue to boil for about 10 to 15 minutes. Stuff each date with an almond. Place dates in a clean, sterilized jar and add a few cloves. Pour in sugar syrup. These dates can be served as a snack along with coffee or tea. Serving size – 2 pieces.

Buttered Dates

1 lb whole dates, pitted
¾ cup butter
⅔ cup flour
1 Tbs cinnamon
Small pinch nutmeg

Place dates in individual dessert dishes. Melt butter over medium heat, whisking to prevent burning. Turn down heat and whisk in flour, cinnamon and nutmeg. Continue to cook another 5 minutes, stirring occasionally. Pour sauce directly over dates and serve warm. Serves 4 to 6.

Sweetened Figs

Juice of 1 lemon
Water
1 tsp grated lemon zest
¼ cup sugar
3 Tbs honey
Pinch of ground cloves
20 walnut halves
20 fresh figs
½ cup plain yogurt
½ tsp vanilla
Chopped walnuts

Combine lemon juice with enough water to make ½ cup liquid. Pour into a saucepan and add lemon zest, sugar, honey and ground cloves. Bring to a boil, then reduce heat, stirring occasionally, until syrup is thick and bubbly. Strain out lemon zest and let cool. Insert a walnut half into each fig. Place figs on a serving platter. Combine syrup, yogurt and vanilla and spoon mixture over figs. Chill and sprinkle with chopped walnuts before serving. Serves 4.

> *I went down into the garden of*
> *nuts to see the fruits of the valley.*
> *— Song of Solomon 6:11*

Salt and
Savory Spices

*Can that which is unsavoury
be eaten without salt?
– Job 6:6*

One of the few substances that the early Hebrews knew
to preserve food was salt. Because there was no refrig-
eration in the biblical era, the only way to preserve
meat was to pack it in salt because salt drew out all
moisture. The main source of salt was the Dead Sea,
which the Hebrews called the "East" or "Salt" Sea.

Many people consider salt the fifth element, because
we depend on it for our survival as much as we do
earth, air, fire and water. The control of such a valu-
able commodity has sparked many a battle – from the
days of ancient Rome to our own Civil War skirmishes.

The Bible mentions it several times, almost always
with reverence and respect. Salt could be purifying. In
2 Kings 2:21, we see Elisha cast it into a barren spring,
"And he went forth unto the spring of the waters, and
cast the salt in there, and said, Thus saith the Lord, I
healed these waters; there shall not be from thence any
more death or barren land."

In the Sermon on the Mount, Jesus reinforces the value
of salt when he says, "Ye are the salt of the earth."
(Matthew 5:13).

And in Colossians 4:6, Paul cautions, "Let your
speech be always with grace, seasoned with salt, that ye
may know how ye ought to answer every man," again
reinforcing the value of salt.

Salt, like honey, was a symbol for rebirth. Newborn

children were ritually rubbed or sprinkled with salt. Salt was used as a substitute for blood in certain rituals to the Hebrew God Yahweh, and altars that had once been blessed with animal sacrifice were later blessed with saltwater or foods seasoned with salt. "And every oblation of thy meat offering shalt thou season with salt; neither shalt thou suffer the salt of the covenant of thy God to be lacking from thy meat offering: with all thine offerings thou shalt offer salt." (Leviticus 2:13)

There was a primitive fear that spilling salt was like spilling blood. Although the action has lost much of its significance, we still throw a pinch of salt over our shoulder as a way of putting the curse of spilled blood behind us.

Besides salt, the Hebrews used dill, mint, hyssop, coriander, cinnamon, saffron and cumin, among a host of other herbs and spices. The phrase "a garden of herbs" is used frequently enough in the Bible that it is obvious household gardens were a prominent feature.

The Last Supper

There has been a long-standing debate regarding the Last Supper: Was it a Passover meal? Because of a slight discrepancy between the Gospel of John and those of Matthew, Mark and Luke, it is unclear which night Jesus and the disciples gathered for their final meal.

John indicates that Jesus was crucified on the day of preparation for the Passover feast, which means the Last Supper the night before could not have been the Passover feast. The other Gospels indicate otherwise. The disciples gathered and "made ready the Passover" and Jesus tells his followers, "With desire I have desired to eat this Passover with you before I suffer: For I say unto you, I will not any more eat thereof, until it be fulfilled in the kingdom of God." (Luke 22:15-16)

So by consensus and long-standing popular tradition, the final meal in which Jesus instituted the Lord's Supper was a Passover meal. What foods would have been at the table?

Hard-Boiled Eggs

These were symbols of the suffering and oppression in Egypt. While most foods become soft in boiling water, eggs only become tougher – just like the Israelites.

Lamb

This is in remembrance of the blood sacrificed.

Bitter Herbs

These are a reminder that the people of Israel were once enslaved.

Greens

These are symbols of Springtime and New Hope.

Salted Water

This is part of the meal in memory of the tears cried in Egypt.

Matzoh

Unleavened bread is eaten in memory of how quickly the Israelites were forced to leave Egypt.

Haroset

This sweet mixture of nuts, fruit, cinnamon and wine has the appearance of straw. It represents the mortar used to build the pyramids.

AT A specific point during the seder, a small amount of haroset is placed on a small piece of matzoh and eaten. The following recipe for Haroset comes from the Middle Eastern, or Sephardic, tradition of Judaism. It reflects the fruits available in that region. Haroset that is part of the Passover celebration in homes of Ashkenazi, or Eastern European, Jews often contains apples rather than dates and raisins, and is usually uncooked.

Haroset

1 lb raisins
½ lb fresh dates, pitted and chopped
2 cups water
1¼ cup sugar
¼ cup chopped pistachios or walnuts

Cover raisins and dates with water and let stand for 1 hour. Add sugar and coarsely chop mixture in a food processor. Transfer to stove and simmer approximately 20 minutes. When cool, stir in nuts.

Scripture Cake

This is not a Bible-era recipe, but a chance to test your scriptural knowledge. The recipe has been passed around for generations. Nobody knows who the original cook was. Some claim it first originated in Europe, others say Colonial America.

See if you can guess the ingredients from the scriptural reference before looking ahead to the contemporary recipe on page 96. Have fun!

> 1½ cups Judges 5:25
>
> 3 cups Jeremiah 6:20
>
> 6 Jeremiah 17:11
>
> 3½ cups 1 Kings 4:22
>
> 2 tsp Amos 4:5
>
> A pinch of Matthew 5:13
>
> Several tsp of 2 Chronicles 9:9
>
> 1 cup Genesis 24:17
>
> 1 Tbs 1 Samuel 14:25
>
> 2 cups dried Nahum 3:12
>
> 2 cups 1 Samuel 30:12
>
> 2 cups slivered or chopped Numbers 17:8

Follow Solomon's advice, Proverbs 23:14.

Scripture References

Judges 5:25

He asked water, and she gave him milk; she brought forth butter in a lordly dish.

Jeremiah 6:20

To what purpose cometh there to me incense from

Sheba, and the sweet cane from a far country? Your burnt offerings are not acceptable, nor your sacrifices sweet unto me.

Jeremiah 17:11

As the partridge sitteth on eggs, and hatcheth them not; so he that getteth riches, and not by right, shall leave them in the midst of his days, and at his end shall be a fool.

1 Kings 4:22

And Solomon's provision for one day was thirty measures of fine flour.

Amos 4:5

And offer a sacrifice of thanksgiving with leaven, and proclaim and publish the free offerings: for this liketh you, O ye children of Israel, saith the Lord God.

2 Chronicles 9:9

And she gave the king an hundred and twenty talents of gold, and of spices great abundance, and precious stones: neither was there any such spice as the queen of Sheba gave king Solomon.

Matthew 5:13

Ye are the salt of the earth.

Genesis 24:17

And the servant ran to meet her, and said, Let me, I pray thee, drink a little water of thy pitcher.

1 Samuel 14:25

And all they of the land came to a wood; and there was honey upon the ground.

Nahum 3:12

All thy strong hold shall be like fig trees with the first-ripe figs.

1 Samuel 30:12

And they gave him a piece of a cake of figs, and two clusters of raisins.

Numbers 17:8

And it came to pass, that on the morrow Moses went into the tabernacle of witness; and, behold, the rod of Aaron for the house of Levi was budded, and brought forth buds, and bloomed blossoms, and yielded almonds.

Proverbs 23:14

Thou shalt beat him with the rod, and shalt deliver his soul from hell.

Contemporary Recipe

- 1½ cups butter
- 3 cups sugar
- 6 eggs
- 3½ cups flour
- 2 tsp baking powder
- 1 tsp each ground nutmeg, cloves and cinnamon
- A pinch of salt
- 1 cup water
- 1 Tbs honey
- 2 cups chopped dried figs
- 2 cups raisins
- 2 cups slivered or chopped almonds

Cream together butter and sugar. Beat in eggs one at a time, beating well after each addition. Sift together flour, baking power, salt and spices. Alternately add flour and water to butter mixture. Add honey, figs, raisins and almonds. Mix well. Turn into two well-greased 9x5x3-inch loaf pans. Bake at 350°F about 60 minutes. Let cakes cool for 30 minutes in pans before turning them out onto a rack. Makes 2 loaves.